ABOUT
NUTS

By Solveig Paulson Russell

Illustrated by Frederick Harris

Melmont Publishers, Inc.
Chicago, Illinois

Also by Solveig Paulson Russell
about Saving Wild Life for Tomorrow
about Trees for Tomorrow
about Fruit
Navaho Land

Library of Congress Catalog Card Number 63-7002

2 3 4 5 6 7 8 9 10 11 12 13 14 15 16 17 18 19 20 21 22 23 24 25 R 75 74 73 72 71 70 69 68 67

TABLE OF CONTENTS

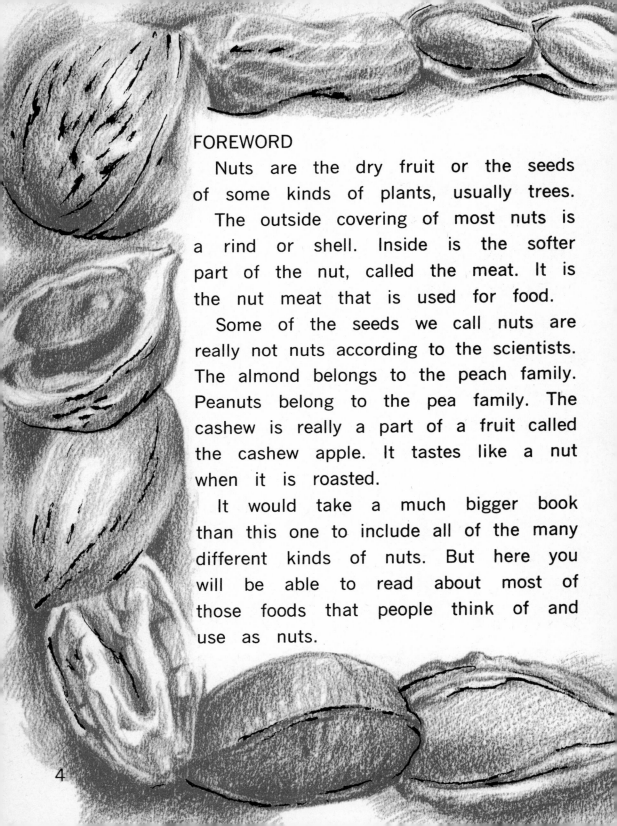

FOREWORD

Nuts are the dry fruit or the seeds of some kinds of plants, usually trees.

The outside covering of most nuts is a rind or shell. Inside is the softer part of the nut, called the meat. It is the nut meat that is used for food.

Some of the seeds we call nuts are really not nuts according to the scientists. The almond belongs to the peach family. Peanuts belong to the pea family. The cashew is really a part of a fruit called the cashew apple. It tastes like a nut when it is roasted.

It would take a much bigger book than this one to include all of the many different kinds of nuts. But here you will be able to read about most of those foods that people think of and use as nuts.

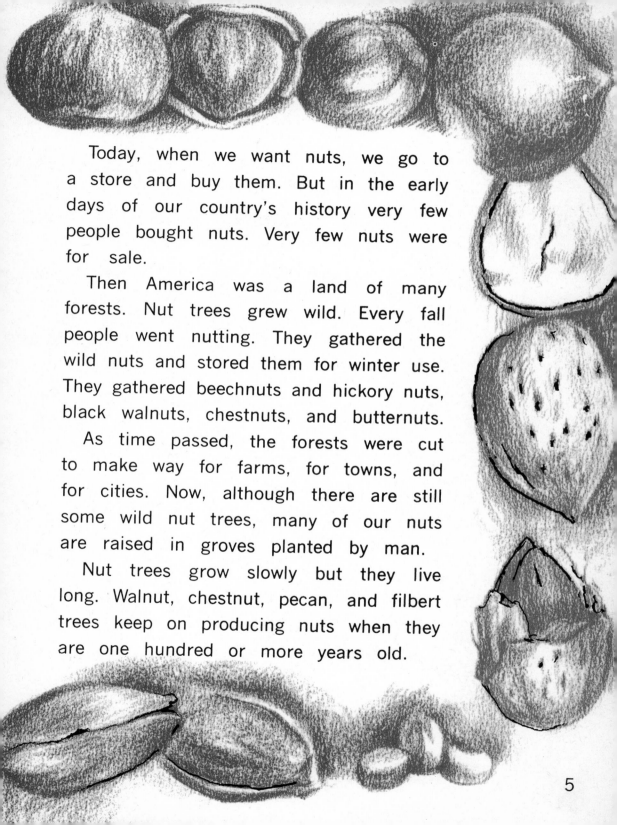

Today, when we want nuts, we go to a store and buy them. But in the early days of our country's history very few people bought nuts. Very few nuts were for sale.

Then America was a land of many forests. Nut trees grew wild. Every fall people went nutting. They gathered the wild nuts and stored them for winter use. They gathered beechnuts and hickory nuts, black walnuts, chestnuts, and butternuts.

As time passed, the forests were cut to make way for farms, for towns, and for cities. Now, although there are still some wild nut trees, many of our nuts are raised in groves planted by man.

Nut trees grow slowly but they live long. Walnut, chestnut, pecan, and filbert trees keep on producing nuts when they are one hundred or more years old.

WALNUTS

There are a number of different kinds of walnuts, among them the English walnut, the black walnut and the butternut.

Walnut trees grow best where the weather is neither very hot nor very cold. The nuts usually grow in clusters. A husk covers the shell of each nut.

Some kinds of walnuts can still be found growing wild; others are cultivated in large orchards or groves. People sometimes have one or more walnut trees in their yards for shade as well as for the nuts they bear.

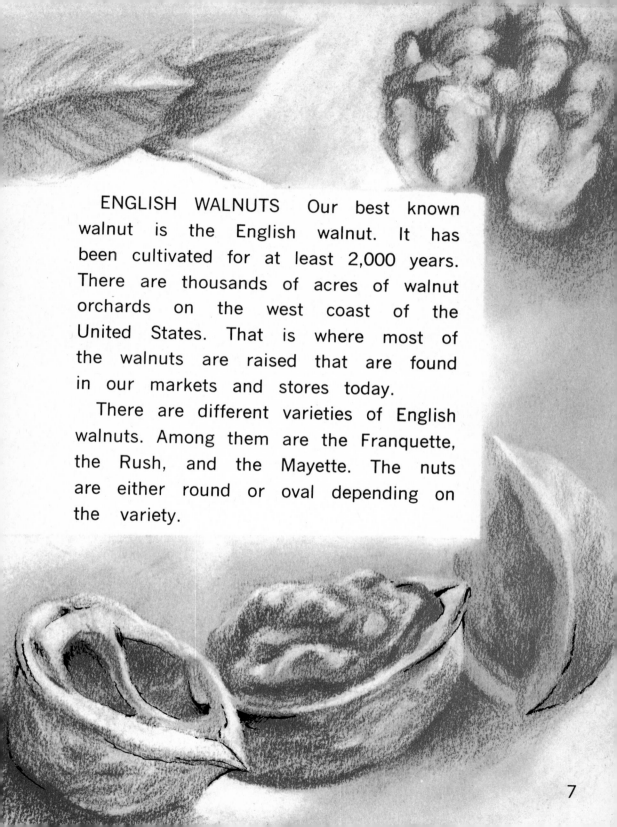

ENGLISH WALNUTS   Our best known walnut is the English walnut. It has been cultivated for at least 2,000 years. There are thousands of acres of walnut orchards on the west coast of the United States. That is where most of the walnuts are raised that are found in our markets and stores today.

There are different varieties of English walnuts. Among them are the Franquette, the Rush, and the Mayette. The nuts are either round or oval depending on the variety.

The shell of the English walnut is somewhat rough. The shell splits easily into halves, which is not true of most other nuts.

As the walnuts ripen, the husks open. The nuts fall to the ground, are picked up, washed, and dried. They are then sorted according to size. Some of the largest and finest walnuts are stamped with a brand name before they go to market. Next time you buy English walnuts, look for the brand name on the shells.

BLACK WALNUTS   Few black walnut trees are raised for commercial use in the United States. Most of them grow wild or are planted in parks and in people's yards.

One reason black walnuts are not used as much as English walnuts is that their thick, green husks do not split open. They must be taken off by hand. Also, the dark shells of these nuts are covered with sharp ridges and do not split into halves as do the shells of English walnuts. The shells are hard to crack and the delicious nut meat does not often come out in very large pieces.

Some growers are trying to develop trees that will produce black walnuts with softer shells. If this can be done, these nuts will probably be used more and will find their way into our markets.

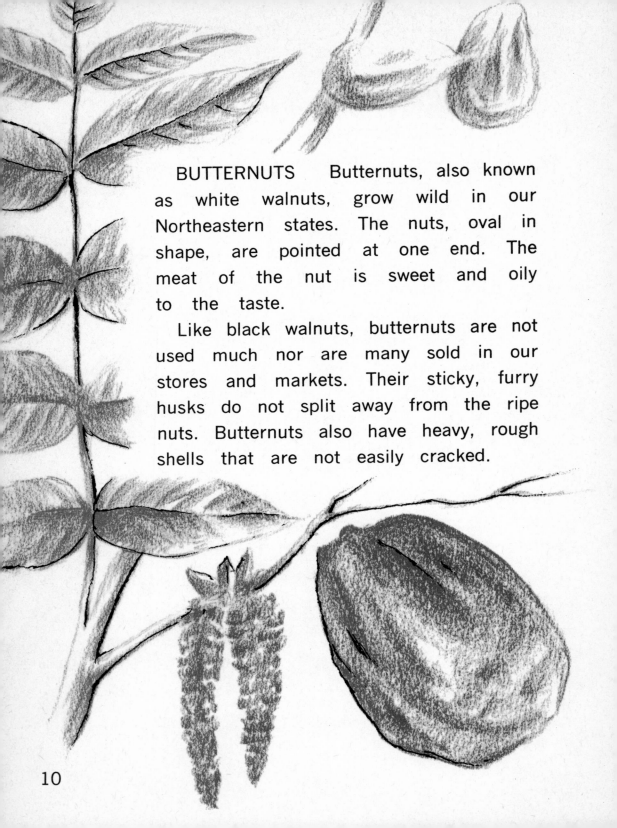

BUTTERNUTS   Butternuts, also known as white walnuts, grow wild in our Northeastern states. The nuts, oval in shape, are pointed at one end. The meat of the nut is sweet and oily to the taste.

Like black walnuts, butternuts are not used much nor are many sold in our stores and markets. Their sticky, furry husks do not split away from the ripe nuts. Butternuts also have heavy, rough shells that are not easily cracked.

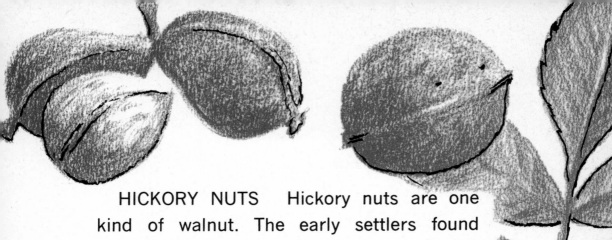

HICKORY NUTS   Hickory nuts are one kind of walnut. The early settlers found hickory trees growing in our astern woods and throughout the South. The Indians gathered and stored these nuts for food before the coming of the white man.

There are several varieties of hickory nuts. The pignut is bitter but the meat of the shagbark, or shellbark, is sweet and good to eat.

When the hickory nuts are ripe, the green husks turn brown. They open and both husks and the light-colored nuts drop to the ground.

The shell of the shagbark is not easily cracked, nor is it easy to get the nut meat out of the shell. This is why it does not pay to raise hickory nuts for the markets. Hickory nuts that reach the markets are from wild shagbark trees.

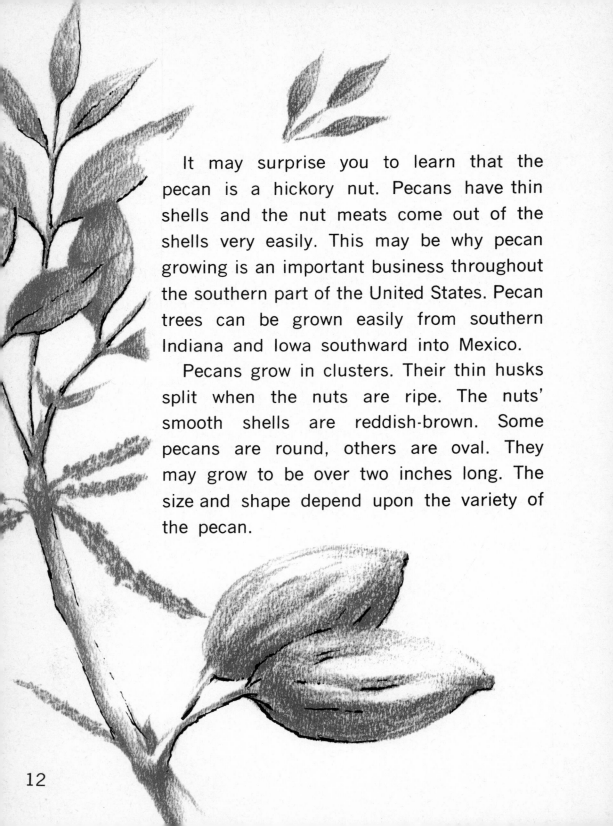

It may surprise you to learn that the pecan is a hickory nut. Pecans have thin shells and the nut meats come out of the shells very easily. This may be why pecan growing is an important business throughout the southern part of the United States. Pecan trees can be grown easily from southern Indiana and Iowa southward into Mexico.

Pecans grow in clusters. Their thin husks split when the nuts are ripe. The nuts' smooth shells are reddish-brown. Some pecans are round, others are oval. They may grow to be over two inches long. The size and shape depend upon the variety of the pecan.

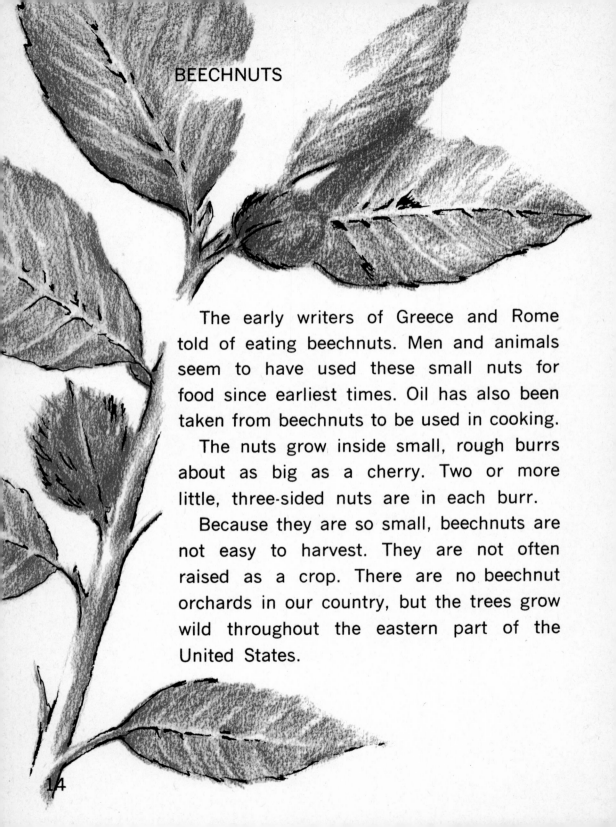

BEECHNUTS

The early writers of Greece and Rome told of eating beechnuts. Men and animals seem to have used these small nuts for food since earliest times. Oil has also been taken from beechnuts to be used in cooking.

The nuts grow inside small, rough burrs about as big as a cherry. Two or more little, three-sided nuts are in each burr.

Because they are so small, beechnuts are not easy to harvest. They are not often raised as a crop. There are no beechnut orchards in our country, but the trees grow wild throughout the eastern part of the United States.

14

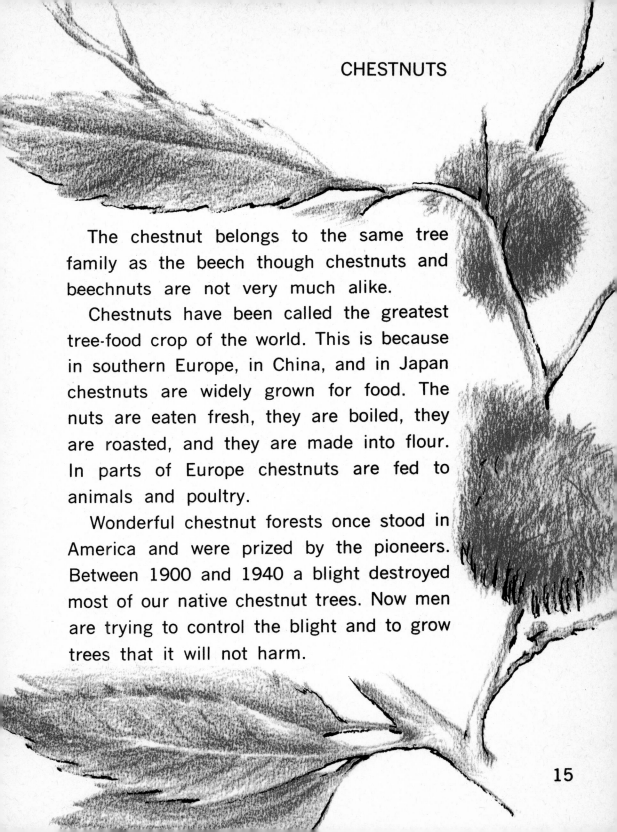

CHESTNUTS

The chestnut belongs to the same tree family as the beech though chestnuts and beechnuts are not very much alike.

Chestnuts have been called the greatest tree-food crop of the world. This is because in southern Europe, in China, and in Japan chestnuts are widely grown for food. The nuts are eaten fresh, they are boiled, they are roasted, and they are made into flour. In parts of Europe chestnuts are fed to animals and poultry.

Wonderful chestnut forests once stood in America and were prized by the pioneers. Between 1900 and 1940 a blight destroyed most of our native chestnut trees. Now men are trying to control the blight and to grow trees that it will not harm.

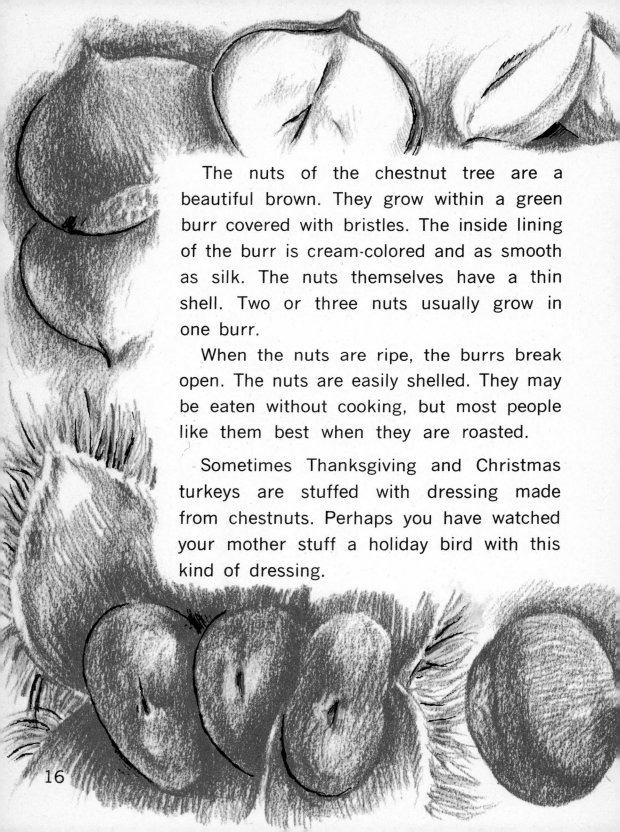

The nuts of the chestnut tree are a beautiful brown. They grow within a green burr covered with bristles. The inside lining of the burr is cream-colored and as smooth as silk. The nuts themselves have a thin shell. Two or three nuts usually grow in one burr.

When the nuts are ripe, the burrs break open. The nuts are easily shelled. They may be eaten without cooking, but most people like them best when they are roasted.

Sometimes Thanksgiving and Christmas turkeys are stuffed with dressing made from chestnuts. Perhaps you have watched your mother stuff a holiday bird with this kind of dressing.

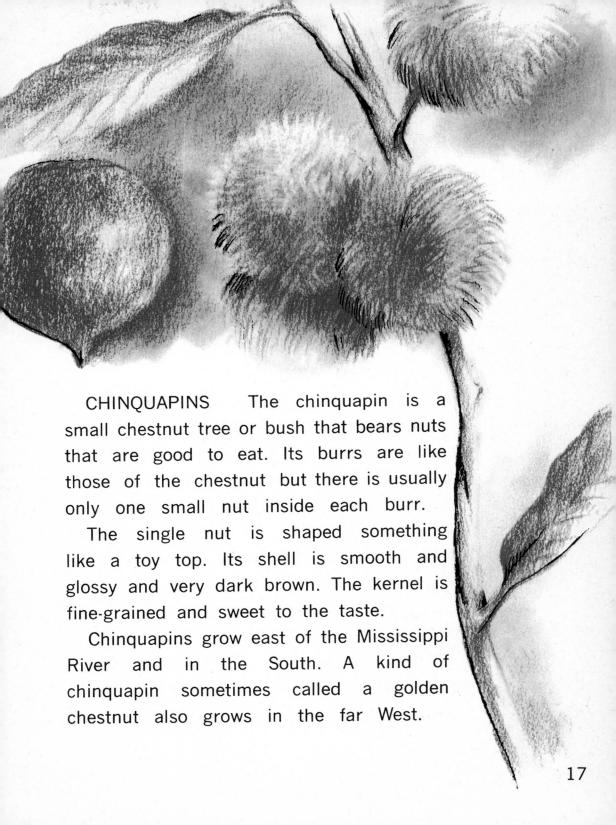

CHINQUAPINS   The chinquapin is a small chestnut tree or bush that bears nuts that are good to eat. Its burrs are like those of the chestnut but there is usually only one small nut inside each burr.

The single nut is shaped something like a toy top. Its shell is smooth and glossy and very dark brown. The kernel is fine-grained and sweet to the taste.

Chinquapins grow east of the Mississippi River and in the South. A kind of chinquapin sometimes called a golden chestnut also grows in the far West.

HAZELNUTS (FILBERTS)

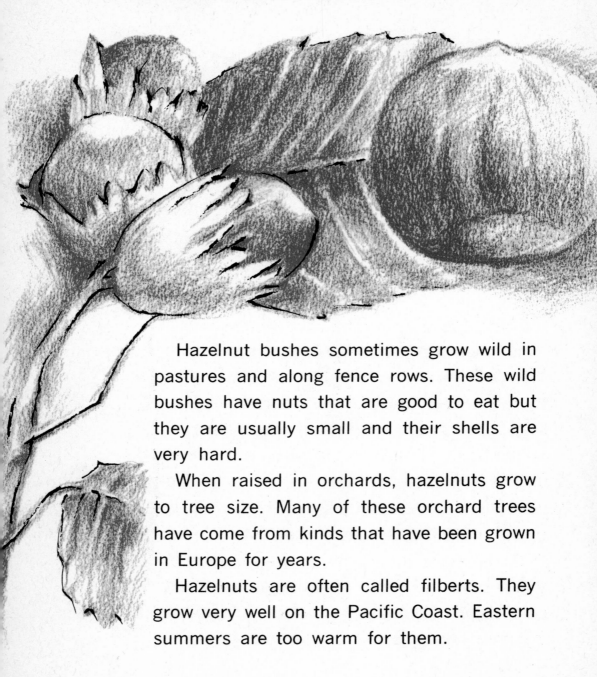

Hazelnut bushes sometimes grow wild in pastures and along fence rows. These wild bushes have nuts that are good to eat but they are usually small and their shells are very hard.

When raised in orchards, hazelnuts grow to tree size. Many of these orchard trees have come from kinds that have been grown in Europe for years.

Hazelnuts are often called filberts. They grow very well on the Pacific Coast. Eastern summers are too warm for them.

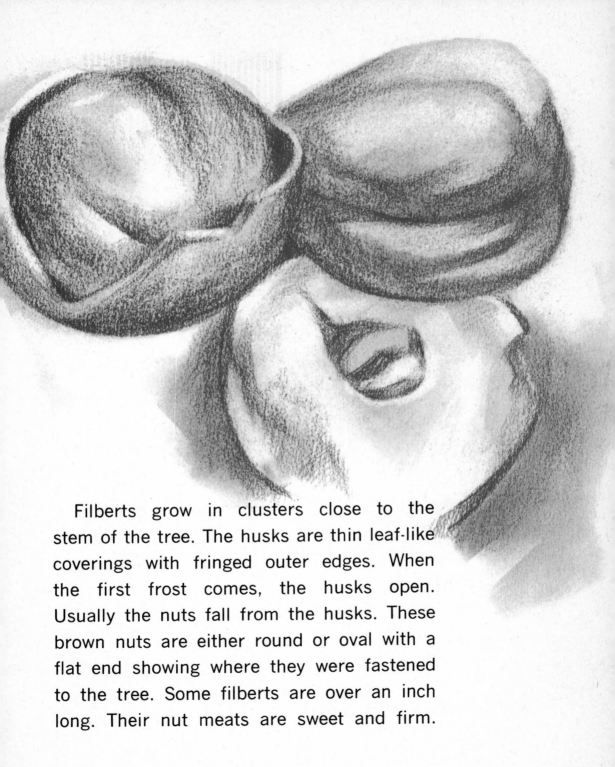

Filberts grow in clusters close to the stem of the tree. The husks are thin leaf-like coverings with fringed outer edges. When the first frost comes, the husks open. Usually the nuts fall from the husks. These brown nuts are either round or oval with a flat end showing where they were fastened to the tree. Some filberts are over an inch long. Their nut meats are sweet and firm.

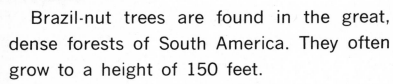

Brazil-nut trees are found in the great, dense forests of South America. They often grow to a height of 150 feet.

The round fruit that holds these nuts is four to six inches through the center. It has a brittle crust on the outside and a tough, woody shell on the inside.

The fruit falls to the ground when the nuts are ripe. It has to be broken open to get at the nuts. As many as twenty nuts are packed inside the woody shell.

The closely-packed nuts are three-sided with rough shells. They are about an inch and a half to two inches long. The nut meats are white, solid, and oily. Those not used for eating are broken up and crushed for making oil.

Brazil nuts are also called cream nuts and Para nuts.

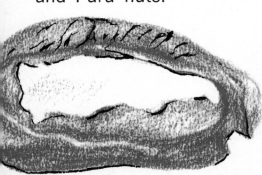

PINE NUTS (PIÑONS)

Pine nuts are the seeds of some kinds of pine trees. They grow in the pine cones, falling out when they are ripe.

Pine nuts are known by several names. The nuts that come from Italy and France are called pinoleas or pignolias. Those from Mexico and our southwestern states are known as Indian nuts, pignons, or piñons.

The pine nuts grown in our country are usually small. They may be as small as a lemon seed; never much bigger than a watermelon seed. In Brazil and Chile, however, pine nuts grow to be as much as two inches in length.

The Indians of the Northwest gathered piñons for food in the early days. Some of them still gather these sweet-flavored nuts.

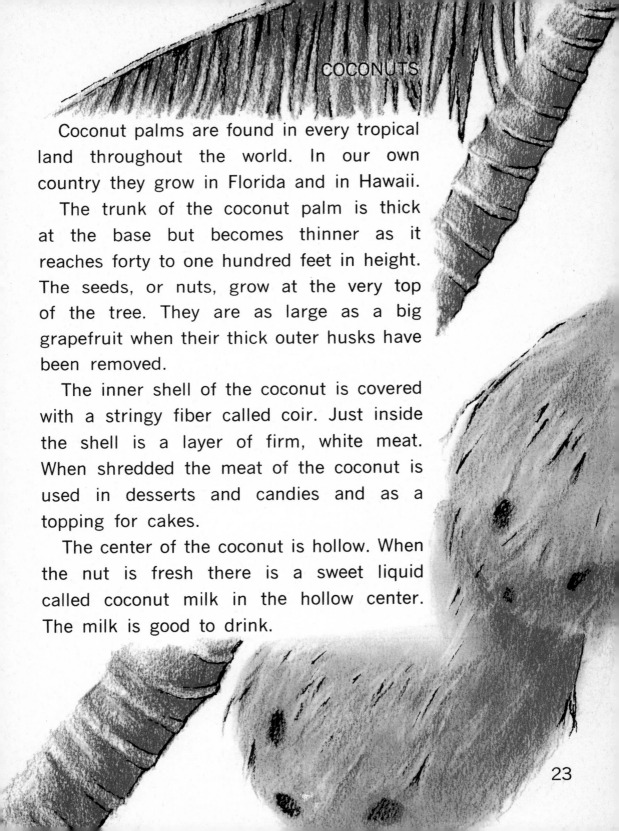

Coconut palms are found in every tropical land throughout the world. In our own country they grow in Florida and in Hawaii.

The trunk of the coconut palm is thick at the base but becomes thinner as it reaches forty to one hundred feet in height. The seeds, or nuts, grow at the very top of the tree. They are as large as a big grapefruit when their thick outer husks have been removed.

The inner shell of the coconut is covered with a stringy fiber called coir. Just inside the shell is a layer of firm, white meat. When shredded the meat of the coconut is used in desserts and candies and as a topping for cakes.

The center of the coconut is hollow. When the nut is fresh there is a sweet liquid called coconut milk in the hollow center. The milk is good to drink.

Coconuts are gathered from wild trees as well as from planted groves. Many people in tropical lands depend upon coconuts for their living. Coconuts are an important crop to many thousands of people.

When coconuts are gathered, the thick husk is removed and the nut meat is broken into pieces for drying. Dried coconut meat is called copra.

It is from copra that we get the shredded coconut used in cooking. Large amounts of copra are used in making coconut oil. When this oil is refined it is pure white. It is used in the manufacture of soap, margarine, and candles. Coconut oil also forms an important part of some face creams and shampoos.

25

ALMONDS

The scientist thinks of the almond as a stone fruit much like the peach. Because most of us know and use only the seed or stone of this fruit, to us it is a nut.

Almond trees look very much like peach trees. In the springtime they are covered with beautiful pink blossoms. The fruit has a fuzzy skin like that of the peach, but the flesh is tough and hard. It is more like a husk than like flesh.

When the husks split, the fruit is ready to be picked. Machines then take the husks from the almonds and dry, bleach, and grade the nuts.

Almonds are somewhat flat and are oval in shape. The shells are so soft they can usually be broken easily with the fingers.

Almonds have been eaten as they come from the shell and have been used in candies and other foods since the days of the Romans.

Marzipan, or marchpane, is a famous candy made from almond paste. You have probably seen marzipan shaped like small fruits and vegetables in places where fine candies are sold. You may even have eaten some of these unusual little sweets.

California is the center for almond growing in the United States.

27

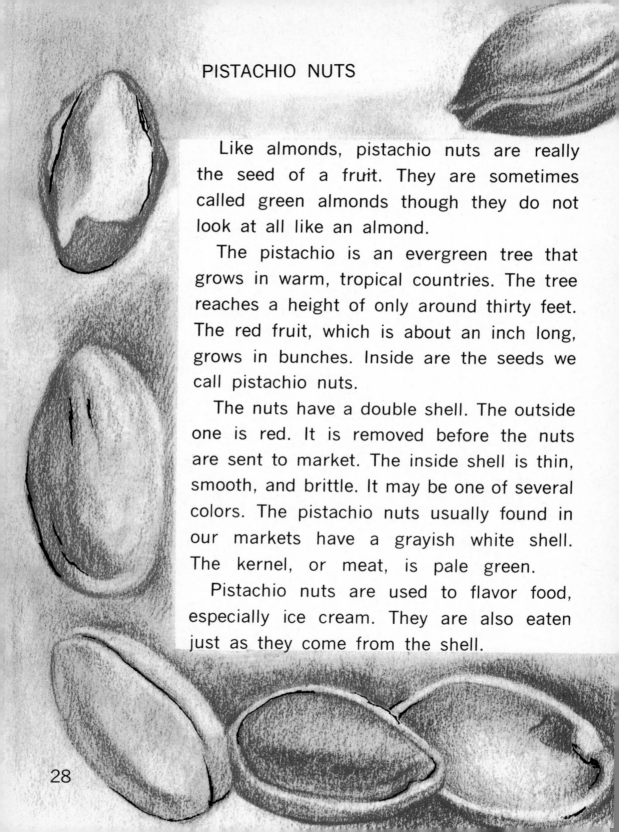

PISTACHIO NUTS

Like almonds, pistachio nuts are really the seed of a fruit. They are sometimes called green almonds though they do not look at all like an almond.

The pistachio is an evergreen tree that grows in warm, tropical countries. The tree reaches a height of only around thirty feet. The red fruit, which is about an inch long, grows in bunches. Inside are the seeds we call pistachio nuts.

The nuts have a double shell. The outside one is red. It is removed before the nuts are sent to market. The inside shell is thin, smooth, and brittle. It may be one of several colors. The pistachio nuts usually found in our markets have a grayish white shell. The kernel, or meat, is pale green.

Pistachio nuts are used to flavor food, especially ice cream. They are also eaten just as they come from the shell.

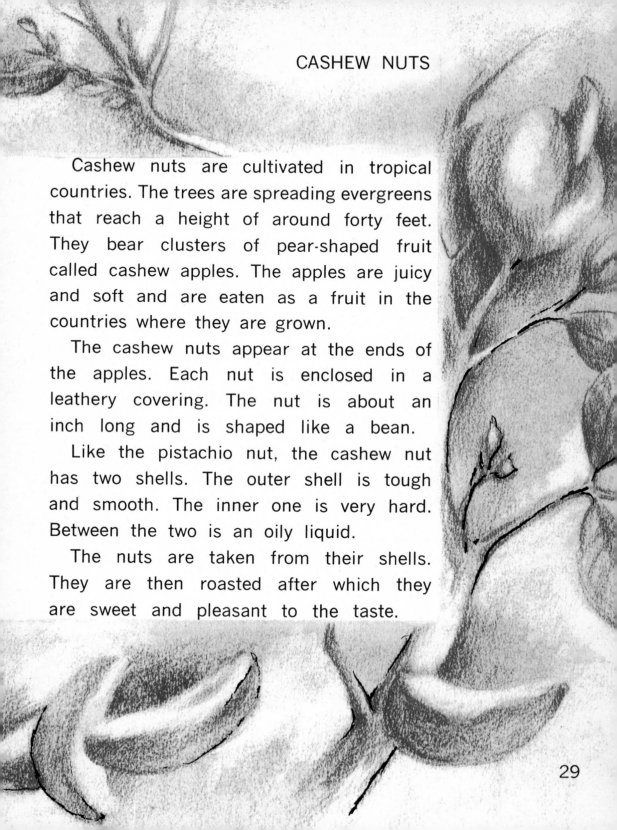

Cashew nuts are cultivated in tropical countries. The trees are spreading evergreens that reach a height of around forty feet. They bear clusters of pear-shaped fruit called cashew apples. The apples are juicy and soft and are eaten as a fruit in the countries where they are grown.

The cashew nuts appear at the ends of the apples. Each nut is enclosed in a leathery covering. The nut is about an inch long and is shaped like a bean.

Like the pistachio nut, the cashew nut has two shells. The outer shell is tough and smooth. The inner one is very hard. Between the two is an oily liquid.

The nuts are taken from their shells. They are then roasted after which they are sweet and pleasant to the taste.

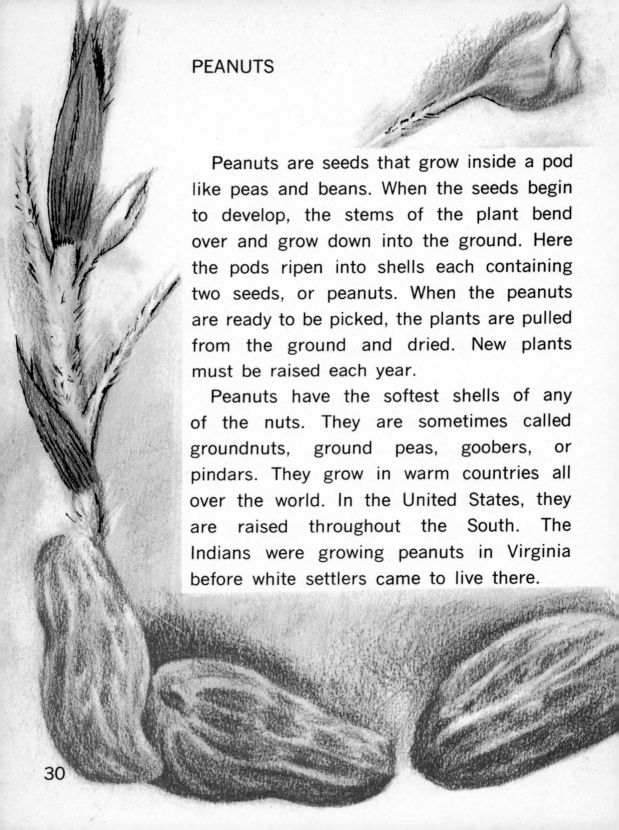

PEANUTS

Peanuts are seeds that grow inside a pod like peas and beans. When the seeds begin to develop, the stems of the plant bend over and grow down into the ground. Here the pods ripen into shells each containing two seeds, or peanuts. When the peanuts are ready to be picked, the plants are pulled from the ground and dried. New plants must be raised each year.

Peanuts have the softest shells of any of the nuts. They are sometimes called groundnuts, ground peas, goobers, or pindars. They grow in warm countries all over the world. In the United States, they are raised throughout the South. The Indians were growing peanuts in Virginia before white settlers came to live there.

We eat roasted peanuts just as they come from the shell. Peanuts are also shelled, then roasted and salted, to be sold in stores and markets. And who is there who hasn't enjoyed a peanut butter sandwich! Peanut butter is made by grinding the nuts.

The oil that can be pressed out of crushed peanuts is used as a cooking oil, for making margarine, and in other products where a vegetable oil is needed.

George Washington Carver, a Southern scientist, discovered more than three hundred ways to use peanuts, their shells, and the peanut plant.

31

Solveig Paulson Russell was born in Utah but has spent most of her life in Oregon. After graduating from the University of Oregon, she taught in both rural and city schools, for the most part in Salem, Oregon, where she now makes her home. Among her hobbies she includes photography, weaving, and wood carving.

Mrs. Russell has been contributing stories and verse to practically all of the magazines for boys and girls for more than twenty years.

A New Yorker by birth, Frederick Harris received his art training at the Art Students' League and the National Academy of Design in New York City, the John Herson Art School in Indianapolis, and the Art Center School in Los Angeles.

Mr. Harris spent four years in the Far East during the Korean War. While there he had two one-man shows in Tokyo. His drawings have also been exhibited in New York City, Indianapolis, and Los Angeles. In addition to being a free-lance advertising artist, Mr. Harris is an instructor at the Art Center School.